I0075054

"ENTREPRENEUR:

STARTING A STARTUP WHEN YOU HAVE NEVER WORKED FOR YOURSELF"

Hello. The very fact that you are reading this right now tells me that you are ready to step out on your own or you at least have a twinkling in your eye of being your own boss and creating a company. If that's the case, gentle reader, please continue.

Let me introduce myself by giving you my bona fides. I hold a BA from Morehouse College in International Studies/Economics. I received my JD from the University of Texas at Austin School of Law. My MBA comes from the Kenan Flagler School of Business or UNC-Chapel Hill. I am the owner of my own private equity firm, Black Wall Street Investments, LLC. based out of Durham North Carolina. I have also operated my own law firm for almost 20 years. My firm reached up to ten lawyers at one time. I was also responsible for bringing in clients and fees for the firm. At one time, my little North Carolina firm represented Duke

Energy, Walmart, Wells Fargo and several other Fortune 500 companies. My problem is that after this and after being a defense attorney in over 100 federal and state major felony trials, I got bored with the law at the age of 45. Now people will tell you that when your back aches in the morning and your hair grows in gray, it's too late to start a new career. I say that simply isn't true. It is never too late to take charge of your life. Running your own business and working for yourself can be a huge part of that.

Purpose:

The purpose of this book is simple: to give you a beginner-basic understanding of what it takes to run your own business. Whether you have worked for yourself or not, in the current environment, it has become hip to call yourself an entrepreneur. It is tough to differentiate yourself from the pretenders in business and make yourself into a contender.

This book will have ten chapters that will be released sequentially so you can understand the beginning steps of starting up your own business.

What this book is:

1. a starting framework for understanding startups;

2.a check list of what you need to start

3. an explanation of basic truths of business that goes all the way back to Adam Smith

Also, this book will provide you with real life interviews with some entrepreneurs who stepped out on their own and made themselves a success or a failure. These insights will be invaluable to you as we go forward. Moreover, here you can access the best interviews and advice from topnotch business professors who strive to make business terminology simpler than you might think.

Lastly, this book seeks to explain the importance of measurables and how they will affect you going forward in your startup.

You have to learn business is not a zero-sum game. You must

learn that hard and smart work is the only way through. You should know the language, the terms that investors throw at you, what they mean and how they can cost you everything if you don't understand them.

IF YOU ARE LOOKING FOR A BOOK TO GUARANTEE YOUR SUCCESS, TRUST ME IT DOESN'T EXIST. THIS BOOK IS TO GET YOU IN THE DOOR AND UP AND RUNNING. TO HELP YOU GET A BASIC PLAN AND FRAMEWORK THAT YOU WILL HAVE TO FILL OUT YOURSELF, BUT THIS BOOK GIVES YOU THE FRAME OF THE BODY THAT YOU CAN TIE THE SINEW AND MUSCLES AND SKIN TO THAT FRAMEWORK START YOUR BUSINESS.

If you are ready to learn, then I'm ready to give you the information you need. It's on you to take the next step forward.

C. Burell Shella, JD/MBA

DEDICATION

This book is dedicated to all those who have ever dreamed of being their own boss and blazing their own trail. Its dedicated to those who have inspired me and stood by me when I want through the growing pains of both of my businesses.

To all those who dream of owning their own successful business and setting the world on fire.

Most importantly, it is dedicated to my wife, son and family.

With Great thanks to Adam Smith " Wealth of Nations", Michael Porter "Five Forces", My professors at UNC and Dr. Willis Sheftall of Morehouse College.

CHAPTER I

HOW TO STEP OUT IN BELIEF
OF YOURSELF

Ok, for you to create your own business you must be able not to just dip your toe in the pool of freedom but splash in with both feet. Now, I know it's a scary thing to leave security for the uncertainty of self-employment; but it's worth the risk.

What are the benefits you ask? According to the SBA in 2010, "... finds that households owning small firms in the 1998-2007 period were more likely than other households to be in the top 50 percent in income and wealth," said Susan M. Walthall, Acting Chief Counsel for Advocacy. Nov. 8, 2010. So, in other words, if you aren't in the top 50% of households you are more likely to be there if you work for yourself.

Moreover, what is the value of setting your own hours? Making your own decisions? Being able to deduct the expenses of your business? How about leaving a business for your children to inherit?

These are just the quick on-its-face reasons to work for yourself. Look, the reality is that you will never generate intergenerational wealth for your family working for a paycheck.

If you want to change an industry or develop your ideas and abilities. You want to work for yourself.

If you want to feel the power of relying on yourself to succeed or fail, then you want to work for yourself.

Lastly, you will never have to worry about the boss yelling at you, denigrating you, lecturing you or firing you. YOU ARE THE BOSS!!! (I do give myself a stern talking to myself in the mirror every once in a while)

Now, what is the downside? Well you are going to burn money at first because it takes time to get a business running. If you have ever heard the adage, you have to spend money to make money? That's exactly what it takes to work for yourself. You are investing in your dream and the future of your family. You may burn through your family savings starting or you may owe investors who divvy up your company if you fail.

Possible failure is another downside. Entrepreneurship is risky. It's possible you put your efforts and money to work only for your business to go down the drain. This could really hurt your feelings and demoralize you. But of course, the jobs carousel will still be waiting on you if you give up on your dream.

Another downside, there is no paycheck security. You will have wild swings of income until you learn to stabilize your cashflow (this will be covered later). If you cannot not tolerate the lack of certainty of income, working for yourself is not meant for you.

What all this comes down to is this. Are you willing to bet on yourself and step out on faith? You have to do it. You must weigh the pros and cons of what you want for yourself and your future. That is a choice you must make yourself.

I ask you to read further so you really need to know what it will require of you to get the business off the ground.

CHAPTER II

STARTING OUT

Now let's to talk about the nuts and bolts of starting your own startup. Now this is a dynamic general list. It will have to be adjusted as you develop your product or by the very nature of what you choose to do. If you are a web designer, you need more advanced technology than a new barber. If you are a storage company, you need more real estate than a photography studio. Please adjust as you develop your idea. Please please do not tie yourself into any long-term leases or agreements as you start out. It could mean doom to you and an

anvil of debt tied to your neck
even after you're ready to move
on to something new.

Technology:

Computer

Ok you are going to need a computer. My advice is to get one that is just dedicated to your business. It doesn't need to be expensive, but it has to have the newest software you can find because you will not have the funds to replace it anytime soon.

Printer

You are definitely going to need a multifunction printer with scanning capability. Scanning and emailing is rapidly replacing faxing as a way of transmitting documents.

Office Space

You are going to most likely going to need dedicated office space or at least a place or a room in your house that is dedicated to your business. You have to have a place that you walk into that is your workplace. This will let you focus on work and not the rest of the world.

Marketing

This is more important than anything else because if people don't know your business exist then you will never have any customers. I would focus every extra dollar you have on this item. The old phrases are " It pays to advertise" but conversely you will pay if you don't advertise your business.

Internet and cellphone/phone number

Comparison shop!!! As for a main number, I suggest that you use google or skype for a main phone number, so you can always control your own number and you can take advantage of their phone services.

These are the basic nonnegotiable items. If you can't do this then you should not move forward. It costs to be the boss.

MATH AND SPREADSHEETS

Ok, for some of you this is the bad news. You must quantify your business to see how it is progressing or regressing. In other words, you must use math to measure your business. Why you ask? Why or Why? Well you are in the business of making money. You must be able to quantify what it cost you to deliver a product, so you can see how much you need to charge to make a respectable profit. Moreover, if you ever want investors so you can spend other people's money, you want to be able to quantify for them the money you are generating, and they want to analyze what the trajectory of your growth, so they can make at least 3x or more over the life of their investment in your company.

To put it simply, the score counts when you build a business. If you can't measure it, you can't know whether to continue to spend money on the business. or whether to dump it. Your investors will not invest if they can't see growth. Lastly if you don't keep track of your dollars and cents how can you tell if an employee or partner is ripping you off?

WHAT YOU DON'T NEED:

PARTNERS

Now this will vary industry to industry. In a complex industry, partners are necessary. In fact, they are preferred especially if you are looking for outside investments. Investors want to see a diverse team that can carry on if one person becomes incapacitated. Moreover, in a complex organization you need to assign different duties, so the business can grow. You need a tech person, a strategist, an accountant, and marketing person.

If your business is much simpler, say opening a garage, or hair salon, or even a law practice. The only thing you prove by bringing on a partner is that two can starve faster than one. You only need to bring in employees when the business is up and running. Anything else will drain the assets of your company and reduce the amount of time you can survive before you become profitable.

LARGE OUTSIDE FUNDING

Now, it's counterintuitive that you would not want large amounts of money to start your business. The important word here is outside funding. If you drown your startup in debt, you will never know its potential because you will have to pay back that money. You cannot predict how your business will do when you first start. Further you may put so much money into it that it is artificially propped up by the investment money.

You also put your ownership in jeopardy when you have private equity or venture capitalist invest in your business. AKA Angel (Devil) Investors. These investors will be discussed in later chapters. Just know dilution is a real possibility.

HEAVY EXPENSES

Entangling you and your family in heavy debt is not the solution. That will make your business grow. When I first started my law practice I went hog wild. Hiring staff, buying expensive furniture, expensive suits and watches. I hung a lot of debt. By the time I realized what I was doing to my practice it took me two years to adjust my cashflow and clear my debt. DO NOT DO THAT TO YOURSELF. YOU WILL REGRET IT!!!!

The key is understanding that early success doesn't equal longevity of success. Your goal is to maintain and grow your business. Now my firm eventually grew & succeeded, but I set its growth back and delayed its growth by not originally plowing the money back into the business where it mattered. You must put money back into your business in places that will increase growth and profit.

ARROGANCE

This is not to say don't be confident but don't be full of hubris (the arrogance of pride). You are beginning in business so there is very little that you probably know about running a business in your new field. I don't mean technical knowledge. I mean practical business of running a business in the field you chose. My law firm became a success because I always asked for help and advice from those that came before me. You would be so surprised about how much your direct competitors would be willing to help you grow.

Please believe me that you must be confident in your work or clients will not have confidence in your product or you. Be humble. Listen. Ask for help. Keep your eyes and ears open.

CHAPTER III:

DEVELOPING YOUR BUSINESS

Economist Michael Porter has defined there are only two ways to compete: price and differentiation. So, you may be asking yourself, what the heck does that mean. Well according to Porters business can either compete to have the lowest price or to have a product is different from its competitors but not on both.

This has been a truism since he announced this theory in the 1980's. Now you may ask yourself, well how about when your product has the exact same price as one company and have more features than another? Well that means that you are competing on price with one company and differentiation with the other. But even with that, you must have a main theory of how you will compete. My favorite example is Costco. Costco competes on price. Period. I know I know they have many products and large portions. But that isn't what they are competing on. Costco is members only club. This makes Costco a service not a product. seller. They aren't Mcdonalds. They don't serve the general public. In fact, they make their profits from their membership not their product sales. "Costco Just Extended Its Advantage Even Further (AXP, COST)"By Investopedia | May 1, 2015.[1]

Probably one of the most well-known example of differentiation competition style is Apple Computers. Apple doesn't care that other companies' computers cost one fourth of the price of theirs. They believe they have a superior product that performs much better than the cheaper products. Since they have become one of the most valuable corporations in the world, it doesn't seem that they are wrong

So, you see, each path can lead to success, but you have to make a decision. For low cost you may have to use inferior therefore cheaper components or if you compete on differentiation you will have to spend more on engineering and features and offer a demonstrable superior product to the competition.

FINDING YOUR NICHE

So how do you find your way?

To start your own business, you need to research the industry and your competition. An example is if you are opening a mid-level full service restaurant you have to check the market. To pick where you place your restaurant you must check the local restaurants in different areas to make sure you aren't overwhelmed with competition. I.E. you don't want to put your restaurant where there are twenty other restaurants that are like yours. Or an area that is too lightly populated, so you have readily available customers.

GETTING HELP

One of the best ways to find help is to locate in a business incubator. These are low cost locations where you will be with like-minded individuals who are striving to start their own business. By associating with them they can give you advice on problems that are making you struggle that they went past in their journey already. Also, many businesses go to these locations to offer their services to startups, so they can get in on the ground floor. So, if the startup becomes successful they can charge them the full freight and grow themselves.

Another route to take is to go to business school or take business courses. Many people are great inventors and great innovators, but I just don't believe that means you are born to be a great businessperson. This is the route I took when I attended Kenan Flagler UNC School of Business. Now I had run my law practice for over 17 years when I started there but my mind was blown by the way I was taught to run my business. The importance of numbers, the importance of projections and how it can be done blew me away. Moreover, to hear the voices of others who had been in business 20 years or more humbled me to the point that I knew I had to listen and grow. You can never truly evaluate the success or growth of your business without real metrics. Doing so will doom you to failure and you will have no idea where to adjust your business.

ADAM SMITH AND COMPARATIVE ADVANTAGE

In 1776, Adam Smith wrote in my opinion the seminal book of Economics. Its truisms are still valid as to this day. To you as an entrepreneur, the most important concept is comparative advantage.

Comparative advantage on a macroeconomic scale is that countries are able to produce certain goods at a lower cost than others. Therefore, every country should concentrate on the goods they could make at better cost and that will cause more worldwide production than if any country tried to produce both products. An example of this is the US has more educated tech workers, so it can build hi tech items at a lower cost than say Cuba.

On the microeconomic scale, a company with a startup founder with an MBA would have a comparative advantage in investments over a farmer who has a comparative advantage at producing apples. So, when you pick, what you want your company to create, you have to evaluate your knowledge and the knowledge of your team so the resources you possess are used efficiently instead of trying to learn a whole new field. A real-world example that you see today is that most companies are divesting themselves of lines of production that they don't do as well as the competition. This takes the drag off of their profitable business and allows them to gain market share in the things they do well

So, find what you do best and exploit it the best you can.

CHAPTER IV

UNDERSTANDING

BUSINESS FINANCIALS

As I have said before, financials are the key to the success of a startup. The tough thing is that the language, terminology and the mathematics of business are not every day common words. I will define some financial terms first then I will talk more directly about how all of these plays together. They are not in any particular order just a non-comprehensive list but it's enough to get you a start.

CASH FLOW- the amount of income you have come in on a monthly basis. It's your life's blood when you work for yourself.

EXCEL- this is a spreadsheet program that will calculate profits and losses when you give it the formula it needs and the data to be calculated. Moreover, it can give you projections of growth and tell the efficiency of your operation

GAAP- Generally accepted accounting practice. This is the prevailing accounting method in the United States. This is the method that either you or your accountant needs to use to keep your books.

PPM- Private Placement Memorandum. This is a document that is required to raise investments from investors of companies. It defines the company, how the money will be invested, and who is responsible for these investments. Don't try and raise money from the general public without it.

ACCREDITED INVESTOR- This is an investor who as a couple make 200k per year of individual making 100k a year or an investment professional

PRIVATE EQUITY- This is an investment company that invest in all sorts of businesses looking for a high rate of return. The key for their role with startups is they provide funds for a percentage of equity of the startup (as a disclosure, I own my own private equity company).

VENTURE CAPITALIST- This is an investor (aka Angel Investor) who invests in a company with taking a promissory note as to their return of their investment.

PROMISSORY NOTE- A loan document that guarantees a venture capitalist his return on investments. It general contains a clause that allows the venture capitalist to force a sale of the startup and its assets to cover its default.

PITCH DECK- a required document for funding it informs investors of what your firm does, who is involved with team and the firm's strategy for growth.

EXIT STRATEGY- Your plan to leave your startup. Investors need to know how they will get their return.

INVESTMENT ROUNDS- these are the stages that you gain financing from different investors. It starts with a seed round and progresses into latter stages.

B2B- business to business

CONVERTIBLE DEBT- a loan that can be converted to equity.

DISRUPTION- changing the game in a particular industry so it is operated differently from that point to ad infinitum.

NON-DISCLOSURE AGREEMENT- an agreement not to discloses the facts or finances of a company. Generally filed when recruiting investors.

ROI- return on investment

VALUATION- how much a company is worth

CROWDFUNDING- A recent phenomena where you can go to the general public to find investment. The downside is the general public has invested your company and non-sophisticated investors will constantly contact you about their investments.

Ok, now that you have some understanding of some important terms, here is how you put them to work for you.

I know I don't have to tell you that you need a bank account but you do and it needs to be a business account. Moreover, you need to get accounting software like Quickbooks to keep track of your expenses so you can document them when you file for taxes.

You have to get yourself an office suite that includes excel. It's the only way to create the financial forms you will need to draw investors by producing your pitchbook and financial projections.

Surprise, you can actually raise money before your business is earning any. The key is proof of concept. Proof of concept is the idea that you have established that your product works and has a valid path to market and success. One of those proofs are your financial projections of how your company will grow and become financially solvent. That is easy to do but you must have a justifiable reason for how quickly your company will grow. You can figure out a reasonable rate based on sales and interest by potential and actual customers.

Next you must evaluate how much your company is worth. That is the valuation. A general rule of thumb is assets plus the stage of development of the company and at least 3 to 5 years of projected income.

Lastly, you should create your pitchbook which is how you can tell investors what your business is about. I have attached an abridged version of my own pitchbook as a guide for you in creating your own.

CHAPTER V

BEWARE INVESTORS:
HOW TO TELL A SHARK
FROM A FRIEND

Ok, I know you have heard the old adage " Don't look a gift horse in the mouth". As a startup, you need to understand that investors are not necessarily gift horses especially when you are invested in by Venture Capitalists. Venture capital is what you see on Shark Tank but it is not a glamorous and elegant as they make it seem. Did you ever notice that they almost never want less than 51 percent of your company? Or they only invest when you have already created a market for yourself and it is always a small percentage of what you value your company at? That is what venture capitalist do. They take over your company if you let them and make you an employee in your own company..

Look I don't want to characterize them all that way but you have to be warned. Just because someone offers to invest in you, you need to look that gift horse in mouth. Ask them about the other companies they have invested in and how those companies ended up. I'm not saying that letting someone take over your company is not a valid exit strategy   (the way to capitalize on your hard work and cash out), but if you plan to work and grow you should leave them alone.

BUSINESS LENDING COMPANIES

These companies are definitely the scratch and sniff arm of business funding. I say this because the interest they charge is ruinous to a startup company. If you have a rough patch, these companies don't care. They don't care what your prospects are only that their loan is repaid. Use these companies at your own risk. They will load you with debt and your dream will die.

PRIVATE EQUITY

Now I can't say I'm not biased because this is what I do. I would want to believe that my industry does it better. The key with private equity is that they come in for a share of equity but they only make a profit if your business grows. If you fail they fail. Generally they want take your assets but I can't promise you that. Generally, folks get taken by private equity when they buy a company from them not when the PE company invests.

CHAPTER VI

MARKETING

The old adage to head here is that it pays to advertise!!!! IF a business fails in darkness no one cares or even knows that it happens. I have seen many companies fail because they were waiting for someone to come to them and save them and for customers to come to them. That simply will not happen. You have to be a tireless marketer as a small business person.

I know that a lot of people will tell you that TV or radio are the best ways to go. They aren't. You are the best advertisement for your business which means you need to get off your butt and go to trade shows or bar meetings, or industry shows to get your product out. You need to go to startup seminars and investment opportunities to get a chance to get investment or to get the general public to know about your product or services. Your pitchbook is what goes to possible investors but you have to decide how you will reach your customers.

As an investment company, I reached out to accredited investors through list provided by companies that compile names and numbers. Moreover, I have joined numerous groups of investors and private equity to let them know who I am what I plan to do and how. It is not easy and sometimes its demoralizing

CHAPTER VII

EXIT STRATEGY

Ok, I know you are wondering why this chapter is talking about leaving your baby the business you nurtured grew and struggle and was your life for years, but there generally comes a time that people will pay a successful business more than it is actually worth. When someone will pay you 500k more than your valuation and you can go grow your business and start something new and be a serial entrepreneur. Now, if you don't intend to leave, please make sure you understand the lifestyle of a business before you decide you are some where for life.

When you start a business and it starts successfully you will enter a high period of growth where your business will never grow this fast again as you win contracts business and interest. Then businesses enter a plateau period where there is still growth but very gradual as compared to the start. Then business starts to tail off as your technology becomes outdate or new technology replaces your company. To take a basic view, a new barbershop opens to a young barber he get his friends and family to come to him. He knows the hipper designs and therefore he gains market share. His business maintains as he reaches middle age. His business will decline as he gets older and his clients move away, lose their hair or die and the newest barber on the block will start to gain market share. So if he would have sold his business on growth or plateau he would have made much more money than he would have after the business started to decline.

Serial entreprenuership would be a real alternative to those who have multiple ideas. You see investors when they invest don't look at business ideas as much as they do teams. They look at real successful teams that flow and work together as something worth investigating. They will invest and watch you fail and reinvest if you have a good justifiable with a good team time after time instead of a team with bad chemistry and a good unique idea.

CHAPTER IIX

TEN GOLDEN RULES OF STARTING YOUR OWN BUSINESS

1. **GET A THICK SKIN**- being an entrepreneur is a lonely business and occasionally demoralizing as you hear people say no again and again. The reason you chose this thing is because you want to be your own boss. That means things will not always go your way. Rejection is part of the business so get used to it or you will never succeed.

2. . **PAY ATTENTION TO THE NUMBERS-** You can never succeed if you don't pay attention to your finance and your growth or lack there off. That is what makes you a success or not.

3. **GET A RABBI-** being an entrepreneur can be a lonely thing. Almost no one around you will be doing what you are so it's hard for them to understand what you go thru with the emotional ups and downs of your business.

4.LEARN THE LINGO- NOT UNDERSTANDING EXACTLY WHAT PEOPLE ARE TALKING ABOUT CAN COST YOU MONEY AND YOUR WHOLE BUSINESS. DON'T BE AFRAID TO ASK QUESTIONS AND CONSULT WITH A LAWYER.

5.PLAN A EXIT STRATEGY- Plan on a way to get out of your business with as much profit as possible. Don't run your business into the ground.

6. **REVIEW YOUR FINANCIALS CONSTANTLY-** You must monitor your financials and cash flow constantly. If you don't you cannot monitor how your business is progressing. Also, you need to periodically review your supplier cost and examine cheaper or higher quality alternative depending on your competition strategy.

7. **IF YOU ARE GOING TO FAIL PULL THE PLUG EARLY-** If you see that your business is not performing you need to shut it down and walk away and go for a new idea. If you stay you will be throwing good money after bad.

8. **TAKE QUALITY TIME FOR YOURSELF**- If you try to do this all day every day you will burn out. Go have a bear go out to dinner with your family. Celebrate your family and your life before the law of diminishing returns causes you to damage your business with bad decision making.

9. REMEMBER THAT EVEN THOUGH YOU WANT TO MAKE MONEY ITS NOT THE REASON YOU ARE DOING THIS- The old adage that you will make money if you do what you love you will make money. If you only focus on money you will make short term profit and lose out on the long game which is the point in having a self-sustaining building.

10. **GIVE BACK**-You aren't a success just because of just yourself. Someone helped you get there. Give back. Remember how grateful you were when a successful person took the time to help you, so help someone else starting out.

CHAPTER IX

PORTER'S FIVE FORCES

I have left the most important points for last: Porter's Five Forces. For your company to succeed, you have to understand your competition which are the people that will take your clients from you. First there are the threat of horizontal forces:

1. Established rivals- think you are a retailer and you draw Walmart's attention.
2. Substitutes- something that can be used instead of your product. Think margarine instead of butter

3. New entrants- new companies that enter the market they try to compete with you on price or differentiation.

The other two are vertical.

1.customer's bargaining power- customers' ability to find products at cheaper prices

2.supplier's bargaining power- by being the only provider to supply a necessary element for your product, they have ability to charge the price they want versus a competitive price that you want.

These things are self-explanatory and are the reason you can be a success or a failure. You must pay attention to them or you will never achieve your dream.

CHAPTER X

FINAL THOUGHTS

Living the dream of working for yourself is not unattainable but it is not easy. You must understand the macroeconomic and microeconomic forces surrounding you to understand and find a pathway to success. This book is not a catchall but a reveal of what you confront and the considerations you must take.

Please do not be afraid of competition, you will face that all your life. But if you understand the considerations that this book explains to you, you will have a leg up on your competition. Understanding the market is the most important tool you can have. If your competition doesn't understand his financials or is able to make projections or understand comparative advantage, you have the ability to swamp him. Good luck and good hunting.

APPENDIX A

SAMPLE PITCHBOOK

BLACK WALL STREET
INVESTMENTS, LLC

Executive Summary

Value Proposition

Our Value Proposition is to acquire and invest in minority businesses that have good financial potential but are failing because of poor financial structure or leadership. We offer access to these closely held companies through our extensive contacts

Goals

To raise the capital necessary to acquire these businesses take them over and rehab them. Our first strategy is to acquire approximately 5 banks with branches that stretch from Georgia to New York. The approximate cost of this strategy will be between $50 million and $75 million with an expected immediate gain of $30 million to $50 million in value.

Our Funds

Our funds seek to raise $275,000,000 total.

OUR APPROACH

BLACK WALL STREET

Purchase undervalued minority owned companies and bring them back to maximum profitability through technology and superior management.

We sell our shares to accredited investors who are savvy enough to see the value of what we are working to achieve.

INDUSTRY SECTORS

TECHNOLOGY		MANUFACTURING
FINANCIAL SERVICES		SOCIAL MEDIA
RETAIL		SERVICE INDUSTRY

The sectors Black Wall Street seeks to invest and develop.

STRATEGIC PROCESS

Many firms these days are run by hunches, guesses, and blind faith. Not at BWSI. We make sure decisions are filtered through our multi-step process to foster success.

1

All decisions will be made with an eye on turning businesses into stable companies and profit to the investors. Our consultants are all business professionals trained not just in strategy, but financial analysis as well.

2

All decisions will be based on financial analysis using cash flow analysis, net present value, regression analysis, return on investment analysis, and strategic fit. Quantitative analyses let BWSI plan for profits and growth by providing in-depth view of company financials.

3

All decisions will be made with an eye on turning businesses into stable companies and profit to the investors. Our consultants are all business professionals trained not just in strategy, but financial analysis as well.

STRATEGIC PROCESS

Many firms these days are run by hunches, guesses, and blind faith. Not at BWSL. We make sure decisions are filtered through our multi-step process to foster success.

1

All decisions will be made with an eye on turning businesses into stable companies and profit to the investors. Our consultants are all business professionals trained not just in strategy, but financial analysis as well.

2

All decisions will be based on financial analysis using cash flow analysis, net present value, regression analysis, return on investment analysis, and strategic fit. Quantitative analysis let BWSI plan for profits and growth by providing in-depth view of company financials.

3

All decisions will be made with an eye on turning businesses into stable companies and profit to the investors. Our consultants are all business professionals trained not just in strategy, but financial analysis as well.

103

OUR FUNDS

BLACK WALL ST. EQUITY FUND, LP

This $25,000, micro equity fund, is the first fund launched by BWSI. As a hybrid fund, it will both invest in funds and acquire ownership or interest in ownership of companies that can maximize our client's investments with healthy profits.

BWSI TECH DISRUPT FUND, L.L.L.P.

Launched on August 30, 2016, the tech disrupt fund is focused on investing in tech companies that change the game for technology as we know it. This fund seeks to invest in mid to late stage startups with excellent technology.

CONTACT US

Registered Office
Black Wall Street Investments, LLC
One World Trade Center, 85th Floor
New York 10007
Email Id: info@blackwallstreetinvestments.com

Primary Address
Black Wall Street Investments, LLC
800 Park Office Dr, Durham
North Carolina 27709

www.ingramcontent.com/pod-product-compliance
Lightning Source LLC
Chambersburg PA
CBHW032011190326
41520CB00007B/431

* 9 780983 360056 *